JOURNEY TO
FREEDOM
FACILITATOR'S GUIDE

YMCA OF
MIDDLE TENNESSEE
/SCOTT REALL

NELSON IMPACT
A Division of Thomas Nelson Publishers
Since 1798

www.thomasnelson.com

JOURNEY TO FREEDOM FACILITATOR'S GUIDE

Published by Nelson Impact, a Division of Thomas Nelson, Inc., P.O. Box 141000, Nashville, Tennessee 37214.

Unless otherwise indicated, all Scripture quotations are taken from the New Century Version® (NCV). Copyright © 1987, 1988, 1991 by Word Publishing, a Division of Thomas Nelson, Inc. Used by permission. All rights reserved.

Scripture quotations marked NKJV are taken from *The Holy Bible*, The New King James Version. Copyright © 1979, 1980, 1982, Thomas Nelson, Inc., Publishers.

To find a YMCA near you, please visit the following websites:
United States of America: www.ymca.com/
Canada: www.ymca.ca/eng_findy.htm
Trouvez votre YMCA: www.ymca.ca/fre_findy.htm
England: www.ymca.org.uk/home/directory/default.asp
Australia: www.ymca.org.au

Visit www.restoreymca.org for more information on Restore, a life-changing ministry of the YMCA.

ISBN 1-4185-0591-9

Printed in the United States of America

06 07 08 09 10 VG 9 8 7 6 5 4 3 2 1

CONTENTS

CREATING A SMALL GROUP OF HOPE, HEALTH, AND HAPPINESS

Welcome to the *Journey to Freedom* group study. Thank you for accepting the challenge of leading others along the way on the journey to freedom. Many will safely travel their journeys to freedom because of your willingness to lead. This Facilitator's Guide will aid you in putting together a plan of action to help participants contemplate the process of change.

Contemplation is how we get an idea of the life we've always wanted. This is a difficult task to take on alone. We need a guide. We need a way to pinpoint the broken areas in our lives, the areas in need of change. This is the purpose of *Journey to Freedom*. It will guide you toward a new life and provide some answers to why life may not have turned out the way you planned. Suggestions will be made, but self-examination is how you'll get the most out of this study. The Bible says, "If you want to build a tower, you first sit down and decide how much it will cost, to see if you have enough money to finish the job. If you don't, you might lay the foundation, but you would not be able to finish" (Luke 14:28–29 NCV). This study is a blueprint that will assist you in change. The last thing we want is for you to lay a foundation of change and run out of steam before reaching your goals. So we created this study to help you get off to a strong start on your journey to freedom.

Here are a few things to remember and tools to use as you travel together with your group on this journey.

WHY JOURNEY TO FREEDOM?

Through years of facilitating restorative small groups, Restore Ministries of the YMCA has learned that the number one reason people retreat and drop out of small groups is because of their lack of preparation for change. Change is hard. Often, the results are not what you expect. Change is easily sabotaged by friends, family, and old, persistent habits.

Journey to Freedom was written specifically to prepare people for permanent, Christ-centered change—the kind that transforms lives and helps us reach our full potential.

THE FIVE STAGES OF CHANGE

In his book *Changing for Good*, Dr. James Prochaska identifies five stages that an individual must go through to prepare for change. The Five Stages are:

Stage 1: *Pre-contemplation.* The individual is unaware of problems, but experiences a vague dissatisfaction with life.

Stage 2: *Contemplation.* The individual identifies a problem in his or her life, but is still deciding whether or not to make any changes. (This is the stage in which many people become stuck. In order to move out of this stage, a motivational force is needed.)

Stage 3: *Preparation.* The individual decides that the benefits of changing are worthwhile. In this stage, the individual contemplates various methods of change and moves toward action.

Stage 4: *Action.* The individual actively participates in some type of activity/program to change their behavior.

Stage 5: *Maintenance.* The individual succeeds in changing his or her behavior patterns and, to prevent relapse, now needs support systems that reinforce the positive changes.

In this six-week course, *Journey to Freedom* focuses on the first necessary stages for change—pre-contemplation, contemplation, and preparation. This focus allows the individual to progress from contemplation to a personal plan of action to change his or her life.

GROUP DYNAMICS

A small group can have several different dynamics. Those who make up the group will undoubtedly have differing views of life. Participants may differ philosophically and spiritually on some issues, so remember to keep the focus on how to contemplate change. Try not to get lost in meaningless conversation, because communication is the lifeblood of every small group. For the group to work, we must talk honestly about our lives. But be aware of moments when the group seems to turn into more of a therapy session for one person. Be flexible with the conversation of the group, but try not to let any one person continually dominate the conversation.

Expect some participants to drop out along the way. Some will decide they're not ready to contemplate change or to begin work on a program of change. That's fine. Don't feel like a failure as a leader if this happens in your group. You may have helped them farther along the journey to freedom than you know. It's discouraging when someone drops out, but don't take it personally. Keep in mind what psychologist Carl Rogers said about groups:

> But what is the psychological need that draws people into encounter groups? I believe it is a hunger for something the person does not find in his work environment, in his church, certainly not in his school or college, and sadly enough, not even in modern life. It is a hunger for relationships which are close and real; in which feelings and emotions can be spontaneously expressed without first being carefully censored or bottled up; where deep experiences— disappointments and joys—can be shared; where new ways of behaving can be risked and tried out; where, in a word, he or she approaches a state where all is known and all accepted, thus further growth becomes possible.[1]

Give participants room to grow by keeping them engaged. Make it real. Mix it up. Some will like an analytical approach, while others will relate strongly to the stories in the manual. Try to keep both styles in mind as you lead. Use the points made in the chapters as an outline. Also, tell the stories from the *Journey to Freedom Manual* in an engaging way. You don't have to be overly dramatic, but use some flair. A good resource to help you with this is *The Art of Talking So That People Will Listen: Getting Through to Family, Friends & Business Associates* by Paul Swets. Also, feel free to add your own stories when you feel they will enhance the lesson.

Some participants will hardly ever make direct eye contact with the others in the group, but always look around the room as you speak. It's tempting to look only at those who seem to be listening. But this may make some believe they aren't important to the group. If everyone in the group looks bored, you may need to change your teaching style. Try to engage the participants by seeming to be confused yourself. Ask questions such as, "I don't seem to understand this point of the lesson. Can someone help me understand? How do you interpret this?" People often like to help others find solutions, even when they are unwilling to grapple with their own issues.

Always remember that this journey will be a life-transforming experience for your participants. So stay strong. You are embarking on a journey to help change lives. Pray for the group on a daily basis. Pray for God to give you wisdom, and be joyful on the journey.

PREPARATION

Being well prepared will help alleviate any anxiety you have about leading the group. When we know what we want to accomplish, it helps us stay on track with the lesson plan. Plus, participants will pick up on your lack of preparation, and that could affect their own dedication to the process of change. In extreme cases, it may cause you to lose some participants. If the leader is not committed, why should the participants be? So come to your group prepared to lead them.

PACE THE GROUP

Use gentleness and patience as you pace the progress of the group. Rushing through the lessons might be exhausting for your participants. Have you ever noticed how popular horror movies allow the audience to breathe by using humor on occasion? This keeps the audience from becoming exhausted. So give the group room to breathe at certain intervals by interjecting humor or a reflection. Try to find some kind of meaningful devotional, excerpt from a book, or song to emphasize and complement what you are studying. If you plan ahead, you can also have these resources available if you ever need to slow the pace of your meeting.

Also, watch the pace of the sharing that is going on. If one member is opening up and sharing for long periods of time, try not to let their problems control the group. Tell them, "I would love to continue this discussion with you after the meeting." Then say, "Will that be okay?" This will keep you from appearing uncaring and will give the group permission to get back on track.

Plan your time so that you are able to get through every question in the Facilitator's Guide, but settle for quality of questions and answers over quantity. The goal is to have a productive meeting. Getting through every question in the lesson may seem optimal, but it may not accomplish the goal.

GOAL OF THE GROUP

The goal of the group is to contemplate change, so there will probably be much philosophical discussion among the group members. When we mainly discuss ideas instead of actions, everything seems fluid. So focus on teaching your group how to draw a map to freedom, but don't push them to a destination. Modifying behavior isn't the particular goal of this group. Even though you may see some behavioral changes as you work together, the main goal of your group should be leading your members as they contemplate why they need to change.

Because your small-group members will be grappling with the idea of change, you may feel as though you're not making progress at times. You may not be able to ascertain the success of the group until Session 6. In the beginning, there will be confusion, awkward silence, and polite surface interaction. It will be awkward, but make every effort to let the group own the discussion. Try asking questions without offering answers.

BOUNDARIES

It's very important to establish boundaries in the first week of your group meeting. These are not intended to be stringent rules, but ones that promote courtesy, respect for one another, punctuality, and the desire to contemplate the process of change.

You may want to share the following guidelines with the group for all meetings:

- Confidentiality is the heart of the program.
- Participants are not required to talk, but encouraged to do so.
- Participants are to respect one another and shouldn't judge or correct other participants. All of us are at different places in our issues, beliefs, and recovery.
- We do not give advice, fix, or rescue other participants.

Think of your role as an examiner who gives drivers a road test. You facilitate all areas of the road test, directing and telling the drivers where to go, but you never actually drive the car. In the same way, as leader of this group, you will direct and instruct participants in a certain direction—without actually driving them to their destination. You will facilitate a direction and a vision. And the direction you will continually give is toward contemplating change and identifying the problem instead of the solution. Then in Session 6 you will help them formulate a plan of action.

SKILLS FOR GOOD SMALL GROUP FACILITATION

- *Avoid being the center of attention.* One of the most common concerns of a facilitator is the pressure to be the center of attention. It's tempting to want to fill the silence when the group isn't talking, or to continue discussing a singular point if you don't feel as if you're getting enough response from the members. However, guard against talking too much in your group sessions. Your role as leader is to get the group involved in sharing, to keep the discussion moving forward and on topic, and to make sure that your group is on time and the necessary material is covered. You are there to give direction and guidance to the group, so avoid dominating the group by talking too much in the sessions.

- *Manage the time wisely.* It is important that your group start and end on time. Strive for consistency, beginning in the first meeting by starting and ending on time and continuing that schedule each week.

- *Be aware of your group.* As a facilitator, get to know your group members. In order to help them as much as possible, you need to be aware and in tune with their needs. Pay attention to the members' body language, their actions, and what they are saying and sharing. Assess each participant in their responses and in their openness (or lack of).

- *Don't let a member dominate the group.* Handling "the talker" in your group will require some skill. Be careful, because if one member begins to dominate your group, it can alienate some of the more reserved members. In order to handle this person in your group, think about positioning. Sit beside the indiviual instead of across from them to avoid prolonged eye contact. When presenting a question or topic for discussion, put a time limit on members' responses. If someone runs over their limit, don't be afraid to break in and praise his or her point, but then raise a new question back to the group about what they have shared. Validate the individual's feelings and input, but then focus the discussion. If needed, confront the person in private outside of group and let him or her know that they may be dominating conversation, but never embarrass him or her in front of the whole group.

- *Be a role model.* A good facilitator is simply a model group participant. Be on time. Be prepared. Do your homework. Guard against moodiness. Be consistent. Be positive. Be a good listener. Maintain confidentiality. Be enthusiastic.

- *Allow silence.* Often facilitators can become uncomfortable with silence in group discussion. Just because there is silence does not mean the process is not working. Sometimes it is good to have a moment of silence so that the participants will speak up and start owning the conversation. Do not feel like you have to fill the void. Give the question time to take root. If the group members think you are going to fill the silence then they will learn to wait for you. Let them process the questions and then begin talking. If you find that there has been a considerable amount of time given to answer a question and no one is speaking up, you might ask them why they are silent or move on to another question.

- *Contain the desire to "rescue."* If someone gets emotionally upset or begins to cry and show emotion during the session, avoid anything that could interfere with the member feeling the emotion of the moment. You may want to reach over and hug them, touch them, or comfort them in some way. However, these are simply moments that the person needs to process what they are feeling or thinking. They may just need to talk and get it all out. Let him or her express the emotions and deal with them, even if they are painful. After he or she has finished sharing and is done, then offer a hug if you desire. Thank and affirm the person for their courage.

- *Be discreet with self-disclosure.* One element of being a good facilitator is a willingness to be vulnerable and to share your journey of change in the appropriate times. However, be careful that you do not use the group to deal with your unresolved issues.

- *Recognize your limitations.* It is important that you remember that you are not responsible for the results of your group. You are not responsible to "fix" anyone. You are not a counselor, a therapist, or a minister. You are a mentor, one who is helping guide another down a path that you have traveled before. Each participant is responsible for his or her own life and journey.

DISCUSSION

As you lead, consistently state and reiterate the boundaries of discussion—confidentiality, respect, and the right to pass. Accept what each person has to say without making sudden judgments. Be the primary catalyst toward providing a warm, open, trusting, and caring atmosphere. This will help the group gradually take ownership. But don't hesitate to probe further if you believe it will help a participant discover a problem area in their life. Lead him or her to the problem in such a way that he or she discovers it for themselves. This is the reward of leading a small group.

THE IMPORTANCE OF ACCOUNTABILITY PARTNERS

One of the best tools to help us through the rough times in our journey to freedom is accountability. Often we don't realize how much accountability has influenced and affected our decisions throughout our lives. We are accountable to get to work on time or we may lose our jobs. In school, athletes have to keep their grades up, attend class, and get to practice or they're off the team. In the same way, unless we have some sort of accountability, many of us will not sustain our efforts to change. We need accountability to develop the discipline of sticking with something, especially if it's new to us.

That is why we need accountability partners. Accountability partners are an integral part in keeping us on the path to change and transformation. They pull us out of isolation and encourage our efforts to change. When we are tempted—and we will be tempted—having an accountability partner makes us think twice before succumbing to temptation. Within the framework of the *Journey to Freedom* program, accountability partners provide us with support and encouragement, and help us maintain our boundaries. Accountability partners provide a community of support when times get tough.

ACCOUNTABILITY PARTNER GUIDELINES

At the end of the first meeting, discuss the points above regarding accountability partners. Explain to the group why accountability partners are important. At the end of first session, assign accountability partners within the group. Tell participants that the your expectations are that they connect with their assigned partner at least three times a week—whether it be through a phone call, meeting for coffee, or taking a walk together.

Advise the group in discussions with their accountability partner, they should:

- Discuss the specifics of the change they're trying to achieve;
- Relate how they are doing in spirit, mind, and body;
- Ask their partner about their struggles, problems, and particular difficulties;
- Be considerate of each other's time and situations, and remember that the purpose is to discuss change—make an effort to take the conversation beyond a superficial level.

At the first session, after you assign partners, ask participants to exchange phone numbers and emails. (If everyone seems comfortable with the accountability partner concept and consents, you may want to provide a typed list the second week with everyone's information on it.) At the end of each weekly session, pair up group members to be accountability partners that week. There is no right or wrong way to assign partners. Often, instinct—and God—will guide you as to who needs to connect that particular week.

When possible, assign participants a different partner each week. The purpose of this is to build relationships within the group and unite the group as a whole. As time goes on and the group grows closer, it is likely they'll start calling more than one group member a week—particularly if there's an issue that two members have in common. The facilitator can choose whether or not to participate as an accountability partner as well, especially if there is an odd number in your group.

COMPONENTS OF EACH LESSON

Each *Journey to Freedom* session is designed to run between forty-five and sixty minutes. Be careful not to spend too much time on the opening components. This will leave you with little time for the main points of the session. Be in control of your time.

As you progress, your group may become very involved in discussion on one question. As the facilitator, decide when to move on or when to stay on a topic that your group is really interested in. Depending on what is most important for your group, feel free to emphasize or expound upon certain questions as you discuss.

The components of leading each session are the same throughout. Along with plenty of questions for discussion, in each of the six sessions, you will find these elements for leading your group:

Lesson Goal—The main objective of the lesson.

Facilitator's Notes—Notes that will help you lead the group. Each lesson begins with a description of what the participant may be feeling at this part of the study. It will remind the leader to remain aware of certain perils of facilitating.

Leading the Lesson—Tips on getting started in the lesson.

Freedom Story—An introduction to the day's lesson that may be a personal success story, a story about the YMCA's history, or an illustration to help you see what a life of freedom looks like and how you can live in freedom as well.

Door to Freedom—A warmup question or two that free up discussion and facilitate group interaction. It helps the group think about the big idea of the session.

Contemplating Freedom—Questions for personal application.

Closing the Group Session—Positive and upbeat ideas to help you close each lesson.

WEEK 1

BEGINNING THE JOURNEY TO FREEDOM

LESSON GOAL

To introduce the *Journey to Freedom* concept. As a result of this session, participants will learn that changing their lives begins by first believing that change is possible. This session is about learning how to contemplate change.

FACILITATOR'S NOTES

As you begin, remember what Gerald May said: "When we fail at managing ourselves, we feel defective."[1] Most everyone in your group has failed at managing themselves. Even though their smiles may hide this failure, they still feel it deep inside. So let them know that change is possible. The first hurdle of leading a group like this is to get your participants to believe in the possibility of change. Continue to remind yourself throughout the lesson that most everyone is only contemplating change at this point. Think of them as tourists who are sightseeing. Be their tour guide by describing the terrain, the history of the place, and the unique advantages. This will keep things in a somewhat passive mode. Above all, have fun with this first lesson.

LEADING THE LESSON

Begin by welcoming participants and encouraging them in their decision to be a part of this healing group. Begin to create a group environment that is comfortable, encouraging, and safe. Have an upbeat demeanor. Work hard at creating a group mentality. If you know someone in the group better than others, don't cater to them because it feels safe. Be vulnerable. This will help create the atmosphere you desire. Remember, there will probably be a level of awkwardness the first few sessions as strangers come together to talk about difficulties in their lives. Do your best to establish a connection with each member in the first week.

The first meeting sets the tone for the group's effectiveness. So be optimistic and hopeful. Tell the participants why you chose to lead the group. Endear yourself to them the best you can by being transparent. People will want to know your successes and your failures. Share both. Tell them how you changed or why you failed. Don't come across as a super-spiritual giant or spill your guts at the first meeting by telling all your war stories. There will be plenty of time for self-disclosure. You have six weeks together, and each week we will get more in-depth. Open up about your own life at key moments along the six-week journey. This will let your members know you're going to take the journey with them and will establish you as the stabilizing influence. Remember that the most important meeting is this one. As the facilitator, you will set the tone for the overall environment of your group today. This environment should be comfortable, encouraging, and safe.

The group should define its purpose, which is to help one another contemplate change. You may want to read this definition of *contemplation* to the group:

> Contemplation *is deep spiritual and mental thought whereby we struggle to understand our problems and their causes so we can begin to seek possible solutions.*

(You may want to use this definition at the start of each session.)

TO OPEN THE SESSION:

1. Welcome the participants and commend them on taking this action to pursue change in their lives.
2. Present group guidelines to the participants:
   a. Confidentiality is of the utmost importance.
   b. Group members are not required to talk but encouraged to do so.
   c. Agree to accept each other and to encourage one another.
   d. We do not give advice, "fix," or try to rescue other group members.
   e. Be honest.
   f. Be on time.
   g. Agree to make the weekly meetings and the daily work a priority.

h. Ask if anyone would like to ask a question or add a group guideline. Goal is for the participants to feel safe, secure, and encouraged.

DOOR TO FREEDOM (INTRODUCTIONS)

Ask each participant to share whatever information they are comfortable sharing about themselves with the group. Name, occupation, number and ages of children or grandchildren, where you were born, how you heard of this group, etc. are good places to start. Be sure that you and your co-facilitator (if applicable) introduce yourselves first to increase their comfort level.

A warm up question or two will free up discussion and help the participants break the ice to begin to open up about their lives. This component is a little longer in the first session to help the group get to know one another.

For discussion:

What do you like to do when you have free time?

What brings you great joy?

What is a special talent or skill that you possess?

FREEDOM STORY

Retell the story of Michelangelo and the angel trapped in a block of stone in Day 27:

Michelangelo understood how to live a life driven by vision. When someone asked Michelangelo what he was doing as he chipped away at a block of stone, Michelangelo replied, "Can't you see there's an angel imprisoned in this block of stone? I'm working as hard as I can to set him free." He first had to envision the angel, and then with his focus on his vision, he worked to set the angel free.

For discussion:

If you were the figure trapped in a block of stone, what would Michelangelo be trying to set free?

CONTEMPLATING FREEDOM

Retell the story about Charles Steinmatz found in Day 2:

Clifton Fadiman tells about Charles Steinmatz, an electrical-engineer genius who worked for General Electric in the early part of the twentieth century. On one occasion after his retirement, they called him in because the other engineers were baffled about the breakdown of a complex of machines. They asked Charles to pinpoint the problem. He walked around the machines for a while, then took a piece of chalk out of his pocket and made a big cross mark on one particular piece of one particular machine.

To their amazement, when the engineers disassembled that part of the machine, it turned out to be the precise location of the breakdown.

A few days later, the engineers received a bill from Charles for $10,000—a staggering sum in those days. So, they returned the bill and asked him to itemize it. He sent one back, which read:

Making one cross mark: $1.00
Knowing where to put it: $9,999.00

Changing our lives always starts with putting the cross mark on the right spot.

For discussion:

If someone instructed Charles Steinmatz to mark an X on the part of your life that is broken, where might he put the X?

Retell the story of trapping monkeys found in Day 3:

A recent television program showed a method for trapping monkeys. The natives made a hole in a log and put bait inside. The hole was just big enough to allow the monkey room to get his opened hand inside the log. So, the monkey reached his hand in to get the bait, but when his fingers closed on it, making a fist, he couldn't get his fist back through the hole. Determined to hang on to what he had, he was still there, trapped by his own greed, when captured. We are much like this monkey when we hold to a life of normality. We fail to do the one thing that would free us, which is to let go and try a new way of life.

For discussion:

Why do we have a hard time letting go of some things, even when we know they are bad for our lives?

Have you ever felt trapped by something you could not let go of? What are some of the things in your life that you feel trapped by?

In Day 4, we read about the history behind using a backboard in basketball:

In 1893, basketball developed a huge problem. Overzealous spectators in the balcony were interfering with the game. They'd reach down and knock the ball away from the basket, infuriating the players and endangering the fairness of the game. Something had to be done about the interference. But what? They could not move the spectators out of the balcony or reposition the goals. So, the search for a remedy soon led to the creation of the first backboard, made out of wire mesh. And it worked. The backboard defended the goal against the spectators who were impeding the game.

For discussion:

Can you name something that has interfered with your attempt to make changes in your life?

Read this story found in Day 5 aloud to the group (Start by asking, "Remember reading about the man trapped in his home by floodwater?"):

As the waters reached his front door he prayed, "God, please rescue me." Ten minutes later, a boat came by, offering to take the man to safety. "No," said the man, "God will save me." The floods rose, and the man, now trapped upstairs, again prayed, "God, please help me." Five minutes later, another boat came, but again the man declined its help. "God will save me," he said, and the boat went away. At last the flood drove the man to the roof where he prayed, "God, please help me." Almost at once a roaring sound hovered above. The man said, "I don't need a helicopter. God will rescue me." The man drowned. In heaven he complained to God about not being rescued, and God replied, "I sent two boats and a helicopter!"

For discussion:
Have you ever responded like the man on his roof when God offers help in ways you weren't expecting?

How do you think being a part of this group will help you understand God's help and presence in your life?

Saint Theresa of Avila said, "The feeling remains that God is on the journey, too." Do you believe this statement? Why? Why not?

Clara, a sixty-three-year-old grandmother whose arthritis prompted her to join the YMCA of Greater Seattle and participate in its programs, took the first step toward reinterpreting her life by joining the Y. She says, "Little did I know how it would change my thinking, my habits, and my outlook on health and fitness. My weight started to drop, and after five months, I had shed thirty pounds. My body image totally changed. I'm still a gray-haired, bespectacled granny with a few extra pounds, but I feel energetic, successful at maintaining my weight, able to lose a few pounds if I choose, and confident I can meet any challenge in my life."

For discussion:

How do you differ from this sixty-three-year-old grandmother?

One of James Naismith's former students, Phog Allen, considered the "father of basketball coaching," told Naismith he was going to Baker University to coach basketball, and Naismith said, "Why, basketball is just a game to play. It doesn't need a coach." But the University of Kansas counts Naismith among its coaches. Evidently, he changed his mind about a coaching career and coached basketball there for nine years. The inventor of the game is the only coach in University of Kansas history with a losing record: 53 wins and 55 losses. How embarrassing! The man who invented basketball could not coach his way to a winning record. But to see Naismith as a basketball failure would be a gross injustice. He invented it. He fathered it, in many ways. So his losing record only makes him human. Everyone has good traits and bad ones. Naismith could have been more creative than administrative. Who knows? But he is a great example of how we live with the tension of both our failures and our successes.

For discussion:

Go around the room and ask participants to name some positives in their lives. Then ask them why they feel this way. This will help end the meeting on an encouraging note.

CLOSING THE GROUP SESSION

- Encourage the group members to come back to the next meeting.
- Encourage group members to read the next week's material and answer the questions at the end of each chapter. Come ready to discuss them.
- Assign accountability partners (explain process/expectations).
- Be sure and thank them for coming this week. Express how excited you are to be with them and to discover where this journey is going to take all of you as a group.
- Close with prayer.

NOTES

NOTES

NOTES

HIDDEN PRISONS:
LIFE-CONTROLLING ISSUES

LESSON GOAL

In this week, we are going to look at the impact that fears, insecurities, and negative thoughts have on our lives. We will discuss why we sink into denial and blame others for our problems. We'll learn to recognize how we've developed patterns of response to negative thoughts and fears. The goal for this week is to eradicate negative, self-destructive thoughts that have developed into permanent and very deeply entrenched behaviors. We will begin to look at how we can move from a place of anxiety to a place of peace.

FACILITATOR'S NOTES

As you begin, remember that most everyone in your group has experienced failure in the past, and their presence in your group displays their determination to change. So be sure to tell them that their problems are only temporary, not permanent. They *can* change. Keep this dangling before them like a carrot because at this point, they are probably unconvinced that they can change. They are certain of their incapacity to become perfect, so they are hoping only for slight changes in their personalities. They are not sure if they can even accomplish this, but they want to stop feeling stuck. Will Rogers once said, "It's great to be great, but it's greater to be human."[1] Let your participants be human.

Here are some definitions that will be helpful:

Inner Critic: The personification of a critical and negative inner voice. It nags and deceives. No matter how we perform, it likes to tell us what we "should" have done, not allowing us to enjoy any success. It makes us feel deeply inadequate.

Procrastination: Another form of denial. It causes us to overlook our problems. Whereas denial is a rejection of the truth, procrastination accepts the truth but delays the action it takes to correct the problem, creating a habitual pattern.

LEADING THE LESSON

1. Start the meeting by welcoming the participants to their second meeting.
2. It will probably be helpful to point out the group guidelines once again:
   a. Confidentiality is of the utmost importance.
   b. Group members are not required to talk but encouraged to do so.
   c. Agree to accept each other and to encourage one another.
   d. We do not give advice, "fix," or try to rescue other group members.
   e. Be honest.
   f. Be on time.
   g. Agree to make the weekly meetings and the daily work a priority.
   h. Ask if anyone would like to ask a question or add a group guideline.
      Goal is for the participants to feel safe, secure, and encouraged.
3. Reread the definition for contemplation and remind the participants that this is the main focus for their sessions:

> Contemplation *is deep spiritual and mental thought whereby we struggle to understand our problems and their causes so we can begin to seek possible solutions.*

FREEDOM STORY

Read the introduction of Day 7 below, and then tell of a time in your life that brings back pleasant thoughts:

I have memories invoked by the hum of lawnmowers in the distance. The smell of fresh cut grass on sidewalks. The sound of a golf club making contact with a golf ball on the greens. All of these remind me of the golf course that loomed before us, as my father taught me how to golf. These were wonderful times.

DOOR TO FREEDOM

For discussion:

Can you tell the group of a time, like Scott's, that brings back pleasant thoughts?

Jerry Seinfeld once said that when at a funeral, most of us would prefer to be in the casket rather than delivering the eulogy. Most of us can relate, because surveys show that we fear public speaking more than death. (Day 8)

For discussion:

Can you tell us of a time when you had to give a public speech that terrified you? How did you get through the speech?

Are you pessimistic or optimistic about your ability to change? Why or why not?

Do you concentrate more on inadequacies than your potential for change?

CONTEMPLATING FREEDOM

Read Dan's testimony to the group (from Day 9):

Dan woke up one day and decided to change. It was as simple and as hard as that. He stood five feet, eight inches tall, weighed 412 pounds, and had been in denial for a long time. Dan said when buying a new car, he didn't compare prices and styles or gas-mile efficiency. Instead, he bought the car that he could fit into. When he frequented restaurants, he asked for a table. Booths were too small, and sitting in chairs with armrests was like being gripped in a vise. He had to ask for seatbelt extensions when he traveled on planes, which stressed him out. He hated his life.

Then Dan purchased a popular book on weight management and began to work out at a Rhode Island YMCA, believing it was not just about diet. This time it was about a lifestyle change. It was about the truth of his condition. It was about getting out of denial.

For discussion:

What do you respect most about how Dan changed his life? Could you do this if you were Dan? If not, why?

Dan says, "I've gotten a lot of people at the end of each group coming to me and saying, 'thank you'. I'm not doing this. They're doing this. Everybody is taking care of themselves. Something that started as a very selfish journey has allowed me to give back to everyone else."

For discussion:

How do we keep from isolating ourselves?

In Day 8 we read:

We find this to be true in the people with whom we work at Restore Ministries. There is a deep-seated fear of inadequacy across the board. Most of them feel that they are not smart enough, good-looking enough, or skilled enough. They say, in essence, If you really knew me, you would reject me. I'm unlovable. So, they go through life waiting on a feeling of absolute certainty. They want to be absolutely certain that no one will reject them before they take any kind of risk. They want to be absolutely certain that they will not fail when they change.

For discussion:

Can we be absolutely sure that this study will work in our lives and produce the willingness to change?

Do you struggle with fear that if people really knew you they would reject you?

Most procrastinators live six months out. They think, I'm going to do something about this, but let's just give it six more months to see what happens. We procrastinate because we don't want to confront the truth about ourselves. We don't want to walk down that difficult path, we don't want to do the work, we don't want to endure the pain or the discomfort that usually comes with change.

For discussion:

Do you think we procrastinate because we don't want to deal with the discomfort of change?

Are you in denial about some issues in your life? Or are you just unwilling to deal with your problem areas?

In Day 10 we read: "Another person in Restore had a dad who berated him and told him he was stupid. 'You're lazy. You can't do anything right.' Over time, he began to believe it. The voice became a hounding inner critic."

For discussion:

Why do we believe things about ourselves that aren't true?

Why do we have an inner critic?

Can it be silenced?

Does the inner critic compare us with others who seem more successful?

When can something in our lives become an addiction?

In Day 11 we read: "When we use addictions as a filtration system in an attempt to cleanse problems from our lives, they only make matters worse."

For discussion:
Do you believe this statement is true or false? Why or why not?

Swimming and aquatics have long been associated with the YMCA, and over the years, tens of millions of people across the country have learned to swim at the YMCA. But this hasn't always been the case. In the early years, swimming suffered at the hands of its critics. Most viewed swimming as a distraction from legitimate physical development. Of course, those critics were wrong.

We should never devalue something until we understand its positive aspects. Always make conclusions about yourself and others by evaluating not only the negative comments, but also the positive ones as well. (Day 10)

For discussion:
How good do you think you are at recognizing the positives and negatives of a situation?

(If you have video access, show the clip of the movie *Castaway* described below.)

In the movie *Castaway*, Tom Hanks stars as Chuck Noland, a workaholic FedEx efficiency expert who knows what it means to control things. He controls his time, his career, his girlfriend, even his thoughts. But all of this changes when his plane crashes in the middle of the Pacific. Noland soon finds himself stranded alone on a remote desert island, unable to control any aspect of his life for five brutal years. And after his rescue, he tells his friend about the time he tried to kill himself while stranded on the island. . . .

Most everyone reaches a moment of clarity when they realize they can't control every aspect of their lives. Human strength is limited. The true source of change happens when we admit we're powerless. (Day 11)

For discussion:
How does admitting you're powerless to overcome your problems help you change?

What in your life are you still trying to control that may be out of your control?

God says, "Come, let us talk about these things. Though your sins are like scarlet, they can be as white as snow. Though your sins are deep red, they can be white like wool" (Isa. 1:18 NCV).

For discussion:
If you had to talk things out with God, what issues would you discuss and why?

In Day 12 we read:

We find this principle in the Lord's Prayer—"Give us this day our daily bread" (Matt. 6:11 NKJV). Our needs are met daily. Instead of obsessing over the future, we need to focus on today. When we take the focus away from ourselves, we will experience real peace—the greatest gift of freedom. It's no longer about relationships that we believe will make us happy or how much money we need in order to be content. It's the realization that choice is at the heart of peace. Freedom is to understand that our happiness is a choice. The one who chooses peace is peaceful. The mind that chooses contentment is content.

For discussion:

Do you believe happiness is a choice?

Can you be happy in all situations?

In Day 12 we read:

If you made a list of the things you wanted out of life, what items would you include? In your youth, you would have no doubt listed some obvious things— beauty, fame, riches, maybe a luxurious car. But as the years go by, you begin to understand more and more that most of these things might not become realities, and even if they do, you realize these things cannot satisfy.

For discussion:

*If you made a list of what you **want** out of life, what items would you list?*

*If you made a list of what you **need** in life, what items would you list?*

Could you live—and be happy—without your wants?

CLOSING THE GROUP SESSION

- Encourage the group members to come back to the next meeting.
- Encourage group members to read the next week's material and answer the questions at the end of each chapter. Come ready to discuss them.
- Assign accountability partners (explain process/expectations).
- Be sure and thank them for coming this week. Express how excited you are to be with them and to discover where this journey is going to take all of you as a group.
- Close with prayer.

NOTES

NOTES

NOTES

CREATING CHANGE

LESSON GOAL

As a result of this session, participants will learn the principles of change. The first principle is that it's impossible to get well on our own. We need others to help us along in the process. The second principle is that we need to experience universality with others in our group. Universality brings a person out of isolation and enables them to get the encouragement, support, and accountability needed for change. By the end of this session, participants will understand how to let go of life-controlling issues that have been holding them back from the lives they've always wanted.

FACILITATOR'S NOTES

You may want to reread the definition of *contemplation* and remind participants that this is the purpose of the group:

> Contemplation *is deep spiritual and mental thought whereby we struggle to understand our problems and their causes so we can begin to seek possible solutions.*

LEADING THE LESSON

1. Welcome the participants back to the third week.
2. If you feel it is applicable, present group guidelines to the participants again:
   a. Confidentiality is of the utmost importance.
   b. Group members are not required to talk but encouraged to do so.
   c. Agree to accept each other and to encourage one another.
   d. We do not give advice, "fix," or try to rescue other group members.
   e. Be honest.
   f. Be on time.
   g. Agree to make the weekly meetings and the daily work a priority.
   h. Ask if anyone would like to ask a question or add a group guideline.
      Goal is for the participants to feel safe, secure, and encouraged.

FREEDOM STORY

Read the story about Robert Roberts in Day 15:

Robert Roberts was a burned-out circus performer. The Big Top no longer thrilled him. He was tired of the spectacular stunts. Tired of the difficult traveling. Tired of all of the same faces, all out for a good time at the show. The thrill was gone in his spirit, mind, and body. And he walked away from it all. But he wanted to continue to stay in shape. So in 1881, Roberts—while on staff at the Boston YMCA—inaugurated a system of exercise he termed bodybuilding work. He believed rigorous repetition of weightlifting could build up the body. But Roberts had no dumbbells, so he used leftover Civil War cannonballs. The workout was a success!

Today bodybuilding, weightlifting, and other individual exercises have become popular in our culture. But most people have a hard time getting motivated to work out. Our minds will play tricks on us. Deceive us. Dissuade us. Keep us in the recliner. It is amazing the excuses we come up with to avoid exercise.

DOOR TO FREEDOM

For discussion:

Can you think of some reasons why people have a hard time getting motivated to work out?

What are the benefits of exercising?

What physical activities do you like to do?

CONTEMPLATING FREEDOM

When we come out of isolation and begin to listen to others, we hear stories of struggle that we thought belonged to us exclusively. It's so freeing to hear that other people struggle too. We realize we aren't alone—and that's *universality*. We begin to open up and feel hope. We feel a sense of companionship and community with others. We're in this together. We all want the same thing—to change and get better.

For discussion:

Have you heard a story from one of your fellow participants that is similar to your own struggle?

How did hearing that person's story make you feel?

Do you believe you can accomplish the change you desire on your own?

Day 14 contains the story about the iceberg that sank the *Titanic:*

If you look at an iceberg, you only see the small portion of ice that is above the surface of the water. The vast majority of the iceberg is underneath the water. In an effort to avoid a head-on collision with the iceberg, the Titanic turned, sideswiping the iceberg beneath the surface and ripping open the hull. Some believe that if the Titanic would have hit the iceberg head-on, there would have been tremendous damage, but the ship might not have sunk. . . .

We have to deal with our problems head-on. Every problem has the possibility to sink us if we try to sidestep it rather than hit it head-on. Beneath the surface of our problems usually looms a greater threat. Drinking, overeating, violent anger, sex addictions, thrill seeking—all of these could be symptoms of something deeper within us.

For discussion:
Can issues beneath the surface sink our lives?

How can we hit our problems head-on?

Do you believe our challenges in life strengthen us and lead us to growth?

For discussion:
Researchers have discovered that most people make efforts of change around their thirty-ninth or fortieth birthday. There must be something about that age. (Day 14)

Why do you think people are motivated to change at this point in their lives?

Long ago, mapmakers sketched dragons on maps as a sign to sailors that they would be entering unknown territory at their own risk. Some sailors would not sail into these unknown waters. Others saw the dragons as a sign of opportunity, as a possibility to discover new territory. Each of us has mental and emotional maps with dragons designating certain areas of our lives. We are not sure what's there. We are afraid to venture out, afraid to look beneath the surface of the dragon. But dragons need to be slain. (Day 14)

For discussion:

In what area of your life are there "dragons," and why are you unwilling to go there?

In Day 16, we read a story about an experiment with monkeys:

A group of business professors once decided to conduct a study with a group of monkeys. What follows is a vivid story of the effects of failure. The professors placed four monkeys in a room with a tall pole in the center. Suspended at the top of the pole was a bunch of bananas. One of the hungry monkeys started climbing the pole to get something to eat, but just as he reached out to grab a banana, the experimenters blasted him with cold water. Squealing, the monkey scampered down the pole and abandoned his attempt to feed himself. Each monkey made a similar attempt and was drenched with cold water. After attempting a few more times, they finally gave up.

The researchers then removed one of the monkeys from the room and replaced him with a new monkey. As the newcomer began to climb the pole to get the bananas, the other three monkeys, who'd tried but failed, grabbed him and pulled him down to the ground. It was a brave act of rescue. They'd tried. They'd failed. They'd felt the cold water in their faces. So, after the new monkey tried to climb the pole several times and was dragged down by the others, he, too, gave up and never attempted to climb the pole again.

The researchers continued to replace the original monkeys, one by one, and each time a new monkey attempted to get the bananas, the other monkeys would again drag him down before he could reach the fruit. In time, the room contained only new monkeys who never attempted to climb the pole for bananas, even though they themselves had never received a cold shower.

Our lives can easily mirror this experiment. We give up on our dreams after a few failed attempts.

For discussion:

Have you ever given up on your dreams after a few failed attempts?

How can you change this?

If you look in the obituaries or on a tombstone, you will see the year the deceased was born and the year he or she died. In between those dates is a dash—representing all the years between birth and death. If I died today, my dash would be between the years 1954 and 2005. But I haven't died yet, so my dash is not complete. But it's possible to lose the urgency of the dash. As some say, "In life there are no dress rehearsals." (Day 16)

For discussion:

Have you lost the urgency of living out your dash?

Jack Welch, longtime CEO of General Electric, says, "Control your destiny or someone else will!"

Has this ever happened to you? If yes, how?

Give an example of how you could control your destiny.

Refer back to the story of Colonel Sanders in Day 17. You may choose to read the story aloud or summarize it.

He dropped out of school at fourteen and tried odd jobs. Became a farmhand and hated it. Tried being a streetcar conductor and hated that. At sixteen, he lied about his age and joined the Army—hated that too. When his one-year enlistment was up, he headed for Alabama, tried blacksmithing, and failed. Then he became a railroad locomotive fireman with the Southern Railroad. He loved this job and wanted to be a railroad man for life. At age eighteen, he married. He had it all: a beautiful wife and a great job. Then failure struck again. The railroad fired him. When he arrived home that day, his wife announced she was pregnant. It seemed to Harland that he could not catch a break. Then one day while he was out job hunting, his young wife gave away all of their possessions and went home to her parents. He felt like a loser and became extremely depressed.

How could an eighteen-year-old have so much baggage so early in life? If this were all the failure he'd face in one lifetime, we would call it a "time of training." But Harland kept losing jobs for various reasons. Then, late in life, he settled into being a "chief cook and bottle washer" at a restaurant in Corbin, Kentucky. He did fine at this job until the new highway bypassed the restaurant and killed the business, and Harland lost what seemed to be his last job. He retired. A lifetime of hope, health, and happiness had evaded him. He had nothing.

Then the postman brought his first Social Security check. That day, something within Harland first resented, then resisted, and finally exploded. He did not want the government feeling sorry for him, and he got so angry that he took that $105 check and started a new business. At the age of eighty-six, he finally became a success. The man who had seemed destined for failure overturned his destiny and got a new lease on happiness, because Harland Sanders—"Colonel Sanders"—started a new business with his first Social Security check. That business was Kentucky Fried Chicken.[1]

For discussion:

Does the Colonel Sanders story offer you hope? If so, how?

What was the key to Colonel Sanders's success?

An old man walked beside his grandson who rode a donkey, as they traveled from one city to another. The old man heard some people say, "Would you look at that old man suffering on his feet while that strong boy is totally capable of walking!"

In the next town, the old man rode the donkey to keep people from thinking bad about his grandson. But then he heard some people saying, "Would you look at that, a healthy man riding a donkey while he makes that poor boy walk!"

This frustrated the man, so he jumped on the donkey behind his grandson.

Now both rode the donkey. But they heard some people say, "Would you look at those heavy brutes making that poor donkey suffer!"

So they both got off and walked the donkey. But then they heard some people say, "Would you look at that waste—a perfectly good donkey not being used!"

So the boy and the old man just ended up carrying the donkey. (Day 18)

For discussion:

Do you believe the people we associate with have an effect on our capacity to change?

Do you believe it's the structure of the program we choose or the relationships we make within the structure that help us change the most?

Do you surround yourself with people who are supportive and encourage you to keep moving forward toward the changes you need in your life?

CLOSING THE GROUP SESSION
- Encourage the group members to come back to the next meeting.
- Encourage group members to read the next week's material and answer the questions at the end of each chapter. Come ready to discuss them.
- Assign accountability partners (explain process/expectations).

- Be sure and thank them for coming this week. Express how excited you are to be with them and to discover where this journey is going to take all of you as a group.
- Close with prayer.

NOTES

NOTES

NOTES

WEEK 4

HOPE RESTORED

LESSON GOAL

As a result of this session, participants will learn that they have a "false self." They will learn why they develop this false self and how it hinders the process of change. Learning to become authentic is the goal.

FACILITATOR'S NOTES

At this point, your group should have a handle on what it means to contemplate change. Now a transition takes place where participants begin to focus on the solutions to their problems instead of denying, blaming, or escaping responsibility for their actions. You will teach them how to focus on the future and let go of past failures as they begin to look at where they want to go, what they would like to see change in their lives, and how to be honest about their life-controlling issues.

Be prepared to move participants closer to God by discussing God's role in their process of change. They will begin to see the hope and encouragement that God provides. With God, there is a promise of transformation and the hope of becoming a new person among others who seek the same change.

Thomas Merton once said, "One of the paradoxes of the mystical life is this: that a man cannot enter into the deepest center of himself and pass through that center into God, unless he is able to pass entirely out of himself and empty himself and give of himself to other people in the purity of a selfless love."[1] This is personal change. When this happens, you'll turn a corner with your group.

Anticipate some excitement as group members begin to see the possibilities that only God can bring to their situations.

LEADING THE LESSON
Congratulate and encourage your members on being back for a fourth week and being committed to this process of change.

FREEDOM STORY
Read the *Peanuts* cartoon story from Day 19:

> A Peanuts cartoon, posted on a ship bulletin board, pictured Charlie Brown and Lucy on a cruise ship. As they stand on the deck, Lucy says, "Life is like this cruise ship, Charlie Brown. Some people take their deck chairs to the front of the ship so they can see where they are going. Other people take their deck chairs to the back of the ship so they can see where they've been. Which one are you, Charlie Brown?"

DOOR TO FREEDOM
Playing off the *Peanuts* cartoon, ask this warmup question: *Are you a "front of the ship" person or a "back of the ship" person? Why?*

Read the following from Day 19 to the group: "We think that if people knew the truth about us, they wouldn't like us. So, we pretend we are someone else, and by doing this, we reject our pain. We stuff it instead of dealing with it."

For discussion:
   What is something that you are afraid of people knowing about you?

   What is something about you that you are proud of, but most people don't know or would be surprised to know about you?

Why do you think we are so afraid of being judged by other people?

What makes it so painful when we feel we are rejected by someone?

If you were to be honest and vulnerable, how do you really feel about yourself?

What do you feel are some of your strongest or best attributes? What do you like about yourself? What makes you special?

CONTEMPLATING FREEDOM

Probe deeper with the following question:

If people knew the truth about you, would they like you?

Jane Fonda calls the false self "disembodiment." In her book *My Life So Far,* she writes, "Because I believed that to be loved I had to be perfect, I moved 'out of myself,'—my body—early on and have spent much of my life searching to come home . . . to be embodied. I didn't understand this until I was in my 60s and started writing this book. I have come to believe that my purpose in life may be to show—through my own story—how this 'disembodiment' happens and how, by understanding it, we can change."[2]

For discussion:

Do you believe being perfect is how we receive love?

Do you pretend you are someone else when you are at church, work, or a party?

Why do you think we do this?

The turning point for Jane Fonda happened in 1998. She made a twenty-minute documentary about her life as a sixtieth birthday present to herself. As she reflected on her life, she had a realization: "The disease to please was in me from an early age."[3] (Day 22)

For discussion:

Why do we live to please other people when it makes us become someone we are not?

Do you need the approval of others to validate your self-worth?

Coach Mike Krzyzewski, Duke University basketball coach, tells a story about the year they won the National Championship. Duke played rival North Carolina and lost by a large margin. The bus ride back to Durham late at night was grueling. When the players got off the bus and started to go back to the dorms, Coach Krzyzewski said, "Where are you going? Let's go practice." Unbelievably, the team's best practice of the year came after that loss—and in the middle of the night.

Coach Krzyzewski said, "People have more of a tendency to listen after a loss, or after they make a mistake. The hardest thing is to have them listen when you're winning. That's why sustained excellence is the most difficult thing to achieve, because you feel like you don't need one another for it."[4] (Day 19)

For discussion:

Do you believe Coach Krzyzewski's statement is true? If yes, why? If no, why?

In Day 20 we read:

When we feel loved in spite of ourselves, it frees us to be more loving toward others. This is why Christ said of the prostitute who washed His feet with her tears and dried them with her hair, "I tell you that her many sins are forgiven, so she showed great love. But the person who is forgiven only a little will love only a little" (Luke 7:47 NCV).

For discussion:

Why would a person love more because they feel forgiven more?

Do you feel valued and loved by God? Why?

In Day 19 we read:

Shame injures our relationships. We cannot experience intimacy if we've closed off our true self. This is why we fall in love with objects. They don't require intimacy. To love houses, cars, jewelry, and other stuff is a false intimacy that never fulfills our loneliness. But we believe if we can just get more and more stuff that it will finally be enough one day. It never is. Objects can never provide the intimacy that we crave so desperately. Relating to the world on this level never makes us feel loved for who we are, but for how we look, perform, or by what we own.

For discussion:

Do you believe the previous statement is true? If yes, why? If no, why?

How can someone overcome a love of objects, so they can pursue real love?

In Day 20 we read:

God's power is not a petulant force or some kind of harsh judgment. It's a relationship. And as we get to know Him more, His life bleeds into ours, the way it does when we fall in love with another human being. We take on His mannerisms. We live to please Him. We want to be like Him. This is how we take on His power. There's more to it than just believing in a higher power. It's a relationship. We accept His love, and He becomes not just an idea or some magical genie to transport us out of our lousy circumstances. He becomes the ultimate Friend and Traveling Companion along our journey to healing.

For discussion:

Do you believe that you can actually have this type of relationship with God?

If you were the last human on the face of the earth, how would your relationship with God change?

How would it stay the same?

Harry Emerson Fosdick wrote, "Watch what people are cynical about, and one can often discover what they lack, and subconsciously, beneath their touchy condescension, deeply wish they had."[5]

For discussion:

Do you think Fosdick's remark is true? Can we really learn what a person feels they are missing in life by listening to what they are cynical about? Why? Why not?

Blues Boy had no indication that this song would be any different. His first seven recordings had flopped, and recording his latest song at the vacant room at the Abe Scharff YMCA in Memphis, Tennessee, didn't add much hope. If anything, it called for even more courage. The recording was cheap and simple—no editing available. It was taped in mono with no room for error, meaning that if Blues Boy and his band messed up, the Ampec reel-to-reel had to start over from the beginning. But, despite the pressure, it only took them two takes to record "Three O'Clock Blues." The song went on to become Blues Boy's first national hit. It remained at number one on Billboard's rhythm-and-blues chart for three months, and from the vacant room in the Memphis YMCA on Lauderdale and Vance, Blues Boy became the man and the legend known as B.B. King.

B.B. said of the song being number one on the rhythm-and-blues chart: "That changed my life."[6]

None of us know when something will come along and change our lives. But B.B. King's recording in the vacant room at the Y proves that sometimes the most unlikely thing in the most implausible place can become a success. If B.B. King had given up after the first seven flops, he would've remained unknown.

Unfortunately, most of us give up before we reach a breakthrough. In America, we spend an estimated $30 billion per year on unsuccessful attempts to sustain a healthy lifestyle. It's astonishing! (Day 22)

For discussion:
What keeps you from maintaining a healthy lifestyle?

Do you struggle with maintaining a healthy lifestyle?

What would you like to change about your lifestyle that would make it healthier?

In Day 23, we read: "[When changing,] take baby steps. You don't have to do it all in one week. Make some small goals, and then accomplish these goals. As you accomplish each one, it will give you more hope. This is what Lewis Smedes means when he says, 'Hope builds on possibilities.'"[7]

For discussion:
If you could take one baby step toward change right now, what would it be?

Dr. Gerald May writes, "Reformation of behavior usually involves *substituting* one addiction for another, adapting to a new, possibly less destructive normality. Sometimes substitution is intentional, sometimes unconscious. An overeater adapts to jogging and yoga; a smoker adapts to chewing gum or eating; a television addict becomes dependent upon guided meditations . . . an alcoholic becomes dependent on AA."[8] (Day 24)

For discussion:
Why is reformation *different from* transformation?

How does understanding this make a huge difference in your process of change?

During World War II, the Nazis set up a camp factory in Hungary where prisoners were made to labor surrounded by barbaric conditions. One day the prisoners were ordered to move a huge pile of garbage from one end of the camp to another. The next day, they were ordered to move the pile back to its original location. No reason was given; they were just told to do it. So began a pattern. Day after day, the prisoners hauled the same mountain of garbage from one end of the camp to the other.

The impact on the prisoners of that mindless, meaningless labor and existence began to come to the surface. One day an elderly prisoner began sobbing uncontrollably and had to be led away. Then another man began screaming until he was beaten into silence. A third man, who had endured three years of labor in the camp, suddenly broke away and began running toward the electric fence. He was told to stop or he would be electrified. He didn't care. He flung himself on the fence and died in a blinding flash.

In the days that followed, dozens of prisoners went insane. Their captors didn't care, for what the prisoners didn't know was that they were part of an experiment in mental health. The Nazis wanted to determine what would happen when people were subjected to meaningless activity. They wanted to see what a life would become without a sense of purpose. They concluded that the result was insanity and suicide. The commandant even remarked that at the rate prisoners were killing themselves, there would no longer be a need to use the gas chambers.

Meaning is decisive to human existence. We all need a purpose. We need to know that our lives matter. (Day 23)

For discussion:
Why is it so hard to discover what our purpose on earth is?

Mother Teresa once said, "What you spend years building, someone could destroy overnight; Build anyway."

For discussion:
What would you like to build with your life?

Would you build anyway if you knew someone was going to come along and tear things down?

CLOSING THE GROUP SESSION

- Encourage the group members to come back to the next meeting.
- Encourage group members to read the next week's material and answer the questions at the end of each chapter. Come ready to discuss them.
- Assign accountability partners (explain process/expectations).
- Be sure and thank them for coming this week. Express how excited you are to be with them and to discover where this journey is going to take all of you as a group.
- Close with prayer.

NOTES

NOTES

OVERCOMING OBSTACLES

LESSON GOAL

As a result of this session, participants will learn how to overcome obstacles and finish their process of change with power.

FACILITATOR'S NOTES

Now we are in the home stretch. Participants in the group have hopefully been honest about their lives and have begun working toward understanding their challenges. They are beginning to see how God can transform lives and do for them what they cannot do for themselves.

In this session, we are looking again at how we need others to encourage us on this journey to freedom. We will encounter setbacks and obstacles. But the vision of the finish line will emerge after this week, and the desire to be set free is going to get stronger. We are getting ready to take action.

LEADING THE LESSON

Thank the members for coming. Congratulate them on how far they've come in their process of change.

FREEDOM STORY

Read the following story from Day 25 to the group:

A few years ago, Restore Ministries planned some small twelve-step groups for inmates at a local prison to help them overcome various problems. I will never forget the chaplain's response to our program. She said that other organizations do short-term work in the prison, which is needed and is much appreciated, but it's only a one-time presentation where inmates are asked, "Who wants to change?" and the inmates raise their hands. But then the presenters leave and have no more contact with the inmates, and it doesn't take long for the inmates to slip back into their old ways. So, the chaplain was thrilled that we were going to aid the other organizations by forming small groups and building ongoing relationships with the inmates. The chaplain understood the powerful dynamics of a small group, which could provide support, encouragement, hope, accountability, love, and nurturing kindness.

DOOR TO FREEDOM

For discussion:

Why are supportive relationships so important for us when we are striving to change our lives?

Who has been a great friend to you in your life—someone who has helped you change or provided for you in a time of need?

What do you like most about your relationships with your closest friends?

Are you good at building relationships?

CONTEMPLATING FREEDOM

Read or retell the following story from Day 25:

Mr. Hatch worked the same drab job in a shoelace factory every day for years. For lunch, he had the same cheese-and-mustard sandwich with a peach for dessert. Everything was the same—day in, day out. He had no friends. He spoke to no one. He went to bed early. He went to the shoelace factory early every day. Then one day he came home from work and received a package from the mailman: a Valentine's Day box of candy with a card that simply said, "Somebody loves you." Mr. Hatch's whole life changed because of this gesture of love. He started his day by speaking to the man at the newsstand when he purchased a newspaper. He began to bake brownies for his neighbors. His outlook on life changed because he had found out that somebody loved him. Then a few days later, the mailman returned to say that he had delivered the box to the wrong address. Mr. Hatch was devastated. He handed over the box with the ribbon attached. Then the card. He watched the mailman deliver the box to the correct house, and then closed his door and proceeded back to his old life. He no longer spoke to the newspaper man or his neighbors. He isolated himself again. He withdrew. Everyone soon noticed that he had changed. They wondered what had happened and what had become of this outgoing, friendly man.

Soon the mailman told them of the mistake. The neighbors shook their heads and then decided to do something about it. One day Mr. Hatch came home from work and a huge banner hung over his apartment door, proclaiming, "Everybody loves you, Mr. Hatch!" He dabbed a tear with his handkerchief. He smiled again. He talked again. The man the neighbors had lost had returned.[1]

For discussion:

We live in a world where it is very difficult to be vulnerable, to be honest, to be who we really are because we fear that we will be rejected. So why bother with love?

Would it be better to live life alone?

Read the following story from Day 26:

One cannot help but be moved by the story of the soldier who asked his officer if he might go out into the "no man's land" between the trenches in World War I to bring in one of his comrades who lay grievously wounded.

"You can go," said the officer, "but it's not worth it. Your friend has probably been killed, and you will throw your own life away."

The man went anyway. Somehow he managed to get to his friend, hoist him onto his shoulder, and bring him back to the trenches. The two of them tumbled in together.

The officer looked down tenderly on the would-be rescuer and said, "I told you it wouldn't be worth it. Your friend is dead, and now you are mortally wounded."

"It was worth it, though, sir," he said.

"How do you mean, 'worth it'? I tell you, your friend is dead!"

"Yes, sir," the boy answered, "but it was worth it, because when I got to him he was still alive, and he said to me, 'Jim, I knew you'd come.'"[2]

For discussion:

Is it possible to find a friend like this soldier outside of our family members?

How can you be a friend like this soldier?

Are friends necessary, or can we go it alone and change without others in our lives?

Should we join a small group? What do you believe are the characteristics of a good small group?

In Day 26 we read: "In Alcoholics Anonymous, they talk about the gift of recovery you receive. They have a saying that to keep recovery, you have to give it away. This is the other benefit of accountability. We will soon be an accountability partner for others. The greatest encouragement we can receive is when God starts using us in other people's lives. It gives us purpose in life."

For discussion:
What do you think about the "gift of recovery"?

Is it plausible?

(If it is possible for you to have video access, show the clip of the movie *As Good As It Gets* described below.)

There is a great scene in the movie *As Good As It Gets* where Melvin (Jack Nicholson) and Carol (Helen Hunt) are having dinner, and she tells him that she is going to leave the restaurant if he doesn't give her a compliment right then. So reluctantly and shyly, he tells her that being around her makes him want to be a better man. What a powerful compliment it was! Whenever we begin to have this type of influence on people, we experience the gift of recovery. We are giving back what we have received from others. And if you've ever wanted to have a positive influence in other people's lives, the way you do it is by respecting them. (Day 26)

For discussion:
Do you believe we can have this kind of impact on other people, to the point where they want to be a better person?

How can respecting other people have a positive influence in their lives?

Do you think we need accountability partners? Why? Why not?

When we live by vision, we don't look only to our past performances. Our focus is on what we *are* going to become, instead of what we *are not* going to be. This is why the apostle Paul said in the Bible, "I know that I have not yet reached that goal, but there is one thing I always do. Forgetting the past and straining toward what is ahead, I keep trying to reach the goal and get the prize for which God called me through Christ to the life above" (Phil. 3:13–14 NCV). (Day 26)

For discussion:

Is it possible to forget the past?

How can we focus on what we can become? Think about Michelangelo chipping from the stone an angel.

Read the following story from Day 29:

There was once a man who knew how to restart after failure. When he was seven years old, his family was forced out of his home on a legal technicality, and he had to work to help support them. At age nine, his mother died. At twenty-two, he lost his job as a store clerk. He wanted to go to law school, but his education was lacking. At twenty-three, he went into debt to become a partner in a small store. At twenty-six, his business partner died, leaving him a huge debt that took him many years to repay. At twenty-eight, he asked his girlfriend of four years to marry him. She said no. At thirty-seven, on his third try, he was elected to Congress, but two years later, he failed to be reelected. At forty-one, his four-year-old son died. At forty-five, he ran for the Senate and lost. At forty-seven, he failed as the vice-presidential candidate. At forty-nine, he ran for the Senate again and lost. At fifty-one, he was elected the president of the United States. His name was Abraham Lincoln, a man whom many consider our greatest leader.

The one thing that remained constant throughout Lincoln's life was the way he restarted after failure. He got back up. He set goals—he achieved some of them and failed at others. But he respected his ability enough to restart time and time again.

For discussion:

When you fail, how long does it take for you to rebound and get started again?

Pretend you failed at a task. What would you say to yourself about this failure?

Do you extend compassion and patience to yourself in all situations?

If you could ask God to help you with one area of your life, what would it be?

CLOSING THE GROUP SESSION
- Encourage the group members to come back to the next meeting.
- Encourage group members to read the next week's material and answer the questions at the end of each chapter. Come ready to discuss them.
- Assign accountability partners (explain process/expectations).
- Be sure and thank them for coming this week. Express how excited you are to be with them and to discover where this journey is going to take all of you as a group.
- Close with prayer.

NOTES

NOTES

NOTES

FINISHING STRONG

LESSON GOAL

This session consists of showing participants how to further their process of change by designing personal plans of action. Making progress in their plans of action will require that they show up, do their part, and trust God with the results. Teach them how to focus on progress instead of perfection. This will give the members determination to stay the course, because recovery is usually two steps forward and one step back. We are constantly a work in progress, so we shouldn't focus on perfection.

FACILITATOR'S NOTES

There should be an atmosphere of celebration and excitement in your group for your last meeting. The members need to be congratulated on starting something and finishing it. For many people who have life-controlling issues and have been in a stage of denial for so long, being a part of this group is alone a huge accomplishment for them.

In this last session, you'll want to warn the members that change always requires some level of risk. As we read in Day 32, "We've got to get out of the boat and walk on the water." Continue to help them fight to gain their freedom by establishing a plan of action. If the participants made it this far, then they are more than likely going to fill out a plan of action. So first help them design their personal plan of change, and then get them to commit to it and be ready to take action.

LEADING THE LESSON

Take a few minutes at the beginning of your session to once again thank your members for their courage to undertake this journey. This is the last session, so work hard to wrap up any loose ends or issues that may need to be addressed at this stage in the participants' journeys. Plan to spend the majority of your time walking the group members through their personal action plans.

FREEDOM STORY

Summarize the Bible story found in Matthew 14.

DOOR TO FREEDOM

For discussion:

If you were in the boat with the disciples, would you be Peter or one of the other disciples who did not risk walking on the water?

What "boat" are you sitting in that you need to get out of to take a risk to change?

Can you recall a time when you took a risk? (Possible answers may include: skydiving, getting married, starting a family, taking a new job, starting a business, etc.)

CONTEMPLATING FREEDOM

In Day 31 we read:

A friend once told me that early in our lives we only know how to get things—but we don't learn how to let go. As we move through our journey to freedom, many of us are going to need to look into our lives and move through the process of grief as we let go and complete the losses of our lives. Then we will be able to dream new dreams and begin to embrace the wonderful gift of Christ's promise: "With God all things are possible" (Matt. 19:26 NKJV).

For discussion:

Why do we need to rescue our hearts from the past?

Are there different types of loss besides death?

Have you had a loss in your life that you feel you need to grieve to be able to move forward?

Read the following story from Day 32 to the group:

Many times we're like the young boy who was doing his best to lift a rock that was too large for someone his size. He grunted and puffed as he tried various methods for lifting the rock. But in spite of all of his efforts, the rock wouldn't budge. His father walked by, and after watching his son's struggle for a few moments, asked if he was having trouble. The boy answered, "Yes, I've tried everything, and it won't move." The father replied, "Are you sure you have tried every possibility, that you have used every resource at your disposal?" The boy looked up with frustration and exhaustion filling his face and grunted out a "Yes!" With kindness, the father bent over and softly said, "No, my son, you haven't. You haven't asked for my help."

For discussion:

Why do we often fail to ask for help? Is it pride or some other reason?

If you could ask God to help you with one area of your life, what would it be?

Thomas Edison gave us—among countless other things—some wise thoughts regarding perseverance. The famous inventor made thousands of trial runs and prototypes before he finally got the light bulb to operate. One day, a workman to whom he'd given a task said, "Mr. Edison, it cannot be done."

Edison said, "How often have you tried?"

"About two thousand times."

"Go back and try two thousand more; you have only found that there are two thousand ways in which it cannot be done."

Edison also said, "Genius is one percent inspiration and ninety-nine percent perspiration."[1] (Day 33)

For discussion:

Do you believe Edison's statement that genius is one percent inspiration and ninety-nine percent perspiration?

Do you believe persevering through trials and tribulations develops strong character? Explain.

Remember the story about the maturing process for bees in Day 34?

Bees go through [a time of struggle] to ensure the healthy development of their young. The queen lays each egg in a six-sided cell filled with enough pollen and honey to feed the egg until it reaches a certain stage of maturity. Then the queen bee seals the capsule with wax. When the occupant exhausts its supply of nourishment, the tiny creature emerges from its confinements. But it wrestles, tussles, and strains to get through the wax seal. And in the agony of its exit, the bee rubs off the membrane that encases its wings—so that when it does emerge, it is able to fly.

For discussion:

What are your reflections on the process of the bee in this chapter?

In what ways do you feel like the bee trying to break the wax seal?

Charles Reynolds Brown, dean of Yale Divinity School (1911–1928), once said, "Everyone is born into the world with a certain unrealized capacity. Let him accept his hand as it was dealt to him, and play the game, without wasting his time bemoaning the fact that his cards are not all aces and faces. Accept yourself for what you are, and for what, by the grace of God, you may yet become, and play the game."[2] (Day 29)

For discussion:
Do you believe that we each are dealt a certain hand and we have to play it as best we can?

In Day 31 we read: "[Stan, a sixty-year-old man,] told me everything over the course of an afternoon. He was on his fifth step in the twelve-step program, the step in which you sit down with one person and share your life story. It's called a personal inventory. The goal is to attempt to answer these types of questions: *Why do I drink? Why do I seek out pornography? Why do I feel rage? Why do I have such a negative self-image? Why am I the way I am?*

For discussion:
At this point in your journey, could you answer these types of questions with someone?

In Day 34 we read:

People who come to Restore usually aren't seeking God. They want to change and improve their lifestyle, their health, and their relationships. They want the pain to stop. But soon they discover that theirs is not only a physical or emotional dilemma, but also a spiritual dilemma. When they realize this, then they are ready to hear God calling them to a place of safety where they can lay their burdens down. Their problem leads them to God.

For discussion:

Do you believe our problems lead us to God or away from Him?

Is God even a factor in your spiritual development?

Do you believe your problem is a physical problem or a mental problem or a spiritual problem?

Do the three areas—spirit, mind, and body—work together to make us whole and free of our burdens and bondages?

CLOSING THE GROUP SESSION

Walk the group together through designing their personal Plan of Change.

BLUEPRINT TO FREEDOM: DESIGNING YOUR PERSONAL PLAN OF CHANGE

Today you will design a Personal Plan of Change. You will set goals in the three areas of change we've discussed—spirit, mind, and body. After defining these goals, you will write out the steps it will take to achieve these goals. Next, you will put together your "Freedom Team," which will consist of the key people who will walk with you along the journey to freedom. They will provide direction, support, encouragement, inspiration, and accountability to help you accomplish your Plan of Change.

First, let's look at a sample Personal Plan of Change.

SAMPLE PERSONAL PLAN OF CHANGE

Self-Assessment: My name is John. I am fifty years old. I am twenty pounds over-weight and have been inactive since college. Every year, I've made New Year's resolutions to lose weight, but I never stick to them. I also have a highly stressful job. I have not been sleeping well, and I know that my eating habits are poor. My alcohol intake has increased over the years, and now I have begun to think about alcohol during the day. When my wife goes to bed, I sometimes sit and drink alone. I'm starting to realize that I haven't thought about having a spiritual life for years. I have become obsessed with the past and the mistakes I've made. I often wake up with a headache and become anxious when I think about going to work. What's wrong with me?

Step 1—Write out your goals.
- *Spirit*—Reconnect with God and build a daily relationship with Him.
- *Mind*—Reduce stress levels and begin to feel a sense of relaxation apart from alcohol. Begin to feel a sense of joy and peace and contentment with life.
- *Body*—Lose twenty pounds by exercising.

Step 2—Take specific steps to meet your goals.
- Spirit: Will get up thirty minutes earlier in the morning and have quiet time reading *My Utmost for His Highest* by Oswald Chambers, and the related Bible verses—and will begin a journal with prayers and thoughts.
- Mind: Will join my friend Bob and attend a Christ-centered twelve-step group at my church.
- Body: Will join a local YMCA and get set up on a personal fitness plan. Will work out four days a week in the morning after my quiet time.

Step 3—Find a support team.
- Support Community: twelve step group, men's group at church
- Individual Support: Bob; sponsor or accountability partner from twelve-step group; pastor at my church; Steve from office as a workout partner

Step 4—Write a brief description of exactly what your life will be like when this change occurs.

There will be a peacefulness that settles in on my life that is not manufactured through any form of mood-altering drug such as alcohol. I will have a personal relationship with God that is the foundational relationship of everything in my life. I will be a better husband and father. I will enjoy my life and my work, seeing it as a part of a greater purpose. Physically, I will have more energy and less stress. Through all of this, I will sleep better, I will feel better, I will look better. I'm looking forward to having a zest for life that has been missing over the past years.

Step 5—Write out a daily prayer to use as you walk the Journey to Freedom.

Dear God, thank You for this day. Thank You for loving me. I pray that Your love overflows into my life and that my life will abound with hope and joy. Give me the strength and courage to follow through to the best of my ability with this plan for today. Guide me into Your will in all that I do. Amen.

Now, it's your turn to write your Personal Plan of Change.

MY PERSONAL PLAN OF CHANGE

Step 1—Write out your goals. For example, if you desire a closer walk with God, then write this in the *Spirit* category below. If you want to learn how to renew your mind by not allowing the inner critic to control you, then write that in the *Mind* category. If you want to lose weight, write that in the *Body* category.

• *Spirit*

• *Mind*

• *Body*

Step 2—Take specific steps to meet your goals:
• *Spirit* (Example: attend church regularly; begin a twelve-step program; spend ten minutes a day in prayer, etc.)

• *Mind* (Example: begin a twelve-step program; contact a therapist)

- *Body* (Example: walk thirty minutes daily; increase fruits and vegetables in my diet; decrease sweets and fats; lift weights three times a week)

Step 3—Find a support team:
- Find a support community. (Choose one of the options below or another group that suits your needs.)

  Restore Ministries
  - Alcoholics Anonymous—*http://www.alcoholics-anonymous.org/*
  - Overeaters Anonymous—*http://www.oa.org/index.htm*
  - Sexaholics Anonymous—*http://www.saa-recovery.org/*
  - Al Anon—*http://www.al-anon.org/*
  - Narcotics Anonymous—*http://www.na.org/*

- Find individuals to support you. (List some individuals below who can support you in your journey.)
  - Friend:
  - Sponsor:
  - Therapist:
  - Counselor:
  - Doctor:
  - Pastor:
  - Life Coach:
  - Personal Trainer:
  - Nutritionist:
  - Physical Therapist:
  - Other:

Step 4—Write a brief description of exactly what your life will be like when this change occurs.

Step 5—Write out a daily prayer to use as you walk the Journey to Freedom.

PERSONAL COMMITMENT TO YOUR PLAN OF CHANGE

The first step in our journey together is wrapping up. We've learned how the change process works, how motivation must be intrinsic to produce change, and that the power to overcome rests in a loving relationship with God. We've learned that we can't make it alone. We need others on this journey. We realize that God has a plan for each step of the way, loving us, strengthening us, encouraging us, and doing for us what we cannot do for ourselves.

Now we approach a very critical point on the journey to freedom. Below is a review of what we've learned. Use it as a reference throughout your journey to gauge your growth and to remember the key points of our study together. You may want to review this list each day.

In this journey, you will need a commitment to live by, as well as something that helps you remember your commitment. Below you will find a list of keys for success in your process of change, and a place for you to sign that you are ready to begin your journey. The journey to real change starts with your signature. For accountability, ask a friend or mentor to sign along with you. Ask them to hold you accountable to this commitment. You're on your way to a lifetime of health, hope, and happiness!

KEYS TO THE SUCCESS OF MY PERSONAL PLAN OF CHANGE

- Maintain an attitude of humility and honesty.

- Don't focus on the problems in the past or perfection for the future. Focus on one day at a time and making the right choices.

- Give yourself permission to get started again on your plan if you slip up, but don't stay in that destructive pattern. If you have no commitment to the plan, then admit it and wait until you're ready.

- Treat yourself with compassion. Learn to be gentle with yourself. Don't internalize mistakes with negative self-talk. Go to God. Go to people on your team. Get the support and affirmation that you need to get back on the plan.

- Learn from your mistakes. What are they teaching you? What can you do to avoid these slips in the future? Let your mistakes be teaching tools, not condemning devices.

- Avoid isolation. Our strengths are in numbers and staying connected to our team and community. Isolation is a dangerous place. None of us has the strength to make it alone.

- Change is about a process and time. Our journeys take time. Be patient.

- Remember, consistency plus time equal change. Take it one day at a time. The new and improved behaviors will come over time.

- Don't make emotional decisions. Use common sense.

- Don't be discouraged if it seems you aren't making any progress. So many people quit because they "feel" they're not changing. Don't make any overall decisions about growth until you are thirty to sixty days into your Plan of Action. Sometimes it takes three or four tries before a plan finally sticks. Again, just keep showing up. Keep coming back and working the plan. The only way we suffer defeat is by quitting.

- Remember, in the end, it's all about coming back to God and just resting in His strength through His grace. He will take care of you.

Dear God,

I, _____, promise, with Your help and with unwavering determination, to follow through with my plan of change to the best of my ability. God, give me strength and courage. Thank You for Your grace and mercy. May Your love encourage me along the way, and remind me to walk this out one day at a time as I focus on my relationship with You. Amen.

_____

(Your signature)

_____

(Signature of a member of your Freedom Team, a friend, or your spouse)

Congratulations! You're on your way!

RESOURCES THAT WILL HELP YOU ON THE JOURNEY TO FREEDOM

Addiction & Grace: Love and Spirituality in the Healing of Addictions by Gerald G. May, M.D.

Changing for Good: A Revolutionary Six-Stage Program for Overcoming Bad Habits and Moving Your Life Positively Forward by James O. Prochaska, Ph.D., John C. Norcross, Ph.D., and Carlo C. Diclemente, Ph.D.

God Will Make a Way: What to Do When You Don't Know What to Do by Dr. Henry Cloud and Dr. John Townsend.

Personal Best: The Foremost Philosopher of Fitness Shares Techniques and Tactics for Success and Self-Liberation by George Sheehan, M.D.

Power to Choose: Twelve Steps to Wholeness by Mike S. O'Neil

NOTES

Introduction: Creating a Small Group of Hope, Health, and Happiness

1. Carl Rogers, *Carl Rogers on Encounter Groups* (New York: Harpercollins, 1970), 11.

Session One: Beginning the Journey to Freedom

1. Gerald May, *Addiction & Grace* (San Francisco: HarperSanFrancisco, 1991), 42.

Session Two: Hidden Prisons: Life-Controlling Issues

1. Zaadz Quote Library, http://www.zaadz.com/quotes/authors/will_rogers/
2. Zaadz Quote Library, http://www.zaadz.com/quotes/authors/hl_mencken/

Session Three: Creating Change

1. Adapted from Paul Harvey, *Paul Harvey's The Rest of the Story* (New York: Bantam, 1978), 115.

Session Four: Hope Restored

1. Thomas Merton, *New Seeds of Contemplation* (New York: New Directions Book, 1972), 64.
2. Jane Fonda, *My Life So Far* (New York: Random House, 2005).
3. Ibid.
4. http://theacc.collegesports.com/sports/m-baskbl/spec-rel/020403aah.html.
5. Dr. Harry Emerson Fosdick, *On Being a Real Person* (New York: Harper Brothers, 1943), 63.
6. B. B. King, *Blues All Around Me: The Autobiography of B. B. King* (New York: Avon Books, 1996), 146.
7. Lewis B. Smedes, *How Can It Be All Right When Everything Is All Wrong?* (Colorado Springs: Shaw Publishers, 1999), 187.
8. Gerald May, *Addictions & Grace* (San Francisco: HarperSanFrancisco, 1991), 147.

Session Five: Overcoming Obstacles

1. Eileen Spinelli, Paul Yalowitz (Illustrator), *Somebody loves You, Mr. Hatch* (New York, NY: Simon & Schuster, 1991).
2. James S. Hewitt, ed., *Illustrations Unlimited* (Wheaton, Ill.: Tyndale, 1988), 226.

Session Six: Finishing Strong

1. Michael P. Green, *Illustrations for Biblical Preaching* (Grand Rapids, Mich.: Baker Books, 1991), 264.
2. Charles Reynolds Brown, *Finding Ourselves* (New York: Harper & Brothers, 1935), 9.